WHAT ABOUT
THE CHILDREN?
200 YEARS OF NORWOOD CHILD CARE 1795 - 1995

WHAT ABOUT
THE CHILDREN ?

200 YEARS OF NORWOOD CHILD CARE 1795 - 1995

THE LONDON MUSEUM OF JEWISH LIFE
AND
NORWOOD CHILD CARE

Published in 1995 by

The London Museum of Jewish Life
and
Norwood Child Care

ISBN 0 9511613 7 7

The London Museum of Jewish Life
80 East End Road
Finchley
London N3 2SY

Norwood Child Care
Norwood House
Harmony Way
London NW4 2BZ

CONTENTS

A NORWOOD CHRONOLOGY   i

RESPONDING TO SOCIAL NEEDS   1

NVEI TSEDEK - THE JEWS' HOSPITAL   3

REPUTATION AND STRUCTURE   7

THE MOVE TO NORWOOD   10

THE JEWS' ORPHAN ASYLUM   15

THE JEWS' HOSPITAL AND ORPHAN ASYLUM   18

GROWTH AND ENLARGEMENT   20

SELECTING THE CHILDREN   22

DEVOTED SUPPORTERS   24

LIFE AT NORWOOD   27

EMPLOYMENT AND AFTERCARE   39

ORPHAN AID SOCIETIES   43

EVACUATION   45

AFTER THE WAR   47

FAMILY HOUSES   51

THE BEGINNINGS OF A COMPREHENSIVE SERVICE   54

NORWOOD CHILD CARE   56

SPECIAL NEEDS   58

NORWOOD TODAY   60

REFERENCES   62

ACKNOWLEDGEMENTS   63

A NORWOOD CHRONOLOGY

1795 **Fund** started for relief of Ashkenazi poor in London.

1807 **Jews' Hospital** (Nvei Tsedek) opened in Mile End "for the reception and support of the aged poor and the education and industrious employment of the youth of both sexes".

1831 **Jews' Orphan Asylum** established "for the maintaining, clothing, educating and apprenticing of Jewish children born in lawful wedlock, deprived of both parents, and for a limited number of one parent only".

1866 **Move to Norwood** - children transferred from Jews' Hospital to new premises at Norwood, South London.

1876 **Amalgamation** of the Jews' Hospital and the Jews' Orphan Asylum to create **The Jews' Hospital and Orphan Asylum** at Norwood.

1883 **Aftercare Committee** established to supervise the welfare of Norwood school-leavers.

1890 **Orphan Aid Society** established to collect funds for the Jews' Hospital and Orphan Asylum.

1897 **Major extensions** to Norwood - Centenary Hall and new wings added to enable the institution to accept more children.

1900 Norwood School under the auspices of **The Department of Education**, leading to improved status and teaching standards.

1911 **Arnold and Jane Gabriel Home** for 50 5-8 years olds opened, increasing the number of children at Norwood to about 400.

1928 Norwood renamed **The Jewish Orphanage**.

1939 **Evacuation** - first to Worthing and then to Hertford.

1945 **Return to Norwood**, with children now attending local schools.

1957 **Norwood Family Houses** established in the neighbourhood between 1957 and 1961, enabling small numbers of boys and girls to live as family grou ps with their houseparents.

1961 **Norwood demolished. New synagogue and assembly hall** built in its place. Shift towards **community-based service**.

1964 Norwood takes on **Highbury House Babies' Home** and other child welfare services formerly provided by the **Jewish Welfare Board**.

1966 Norwood establishes a **Hostel for Unmarried Mothers**.

1970s **Family Houses move** to North London. **Norwood sold**.

Norwood Domiciliary Service established, using Social Workers and Child Development Advisers to support and advise children and families.

1990 Norwood **Jewish Adoption Society** established - the only Jewish adoption agency in United Kingdom.

1990 **Koleinu** ('Our Voice') established - a new project for hearing-impaired Jewish young people and their families.

1990 **Norwood Family Centre** opened in Hendon, offering practical advice and support to families in difficulty.

1992 Last Family House closed. **Adolescent Unit** created.

1993 **Buckets and Spades Lodge**, a respite care home for children with special needs, established as a joint facility with Ravenswood.

1993 **Oakfield Link** set up to provide temporary supported bed-sit accommodation to homeless young adults.

1995 **Alldun**, a second bed-sit accommodation unit, built.

FUTURE PLANS

1995 **Binoh's Special Education Unit**, an expansion at Norwood House, to provide intensive support to children with special educational needs attending mainstream schools.

1995 **Hackney Child and Family Centre**, a multi-disciplinary centre with special educational and social services for Jewish children and families in need of support.

Redbridge Family Centre to develop existing services in the North-East London area.

Additional supported accommodation units, to provide semi-independent bed-sits for young people in need.

RESPONDING TO SOCIAL NEEDS

Norwood Child Care has a long history of responding to Jewish social needs in Britain. It started as a small boarding trade school for the children of poor members of the Jewish community. Through amalgamation, growth and diversification, it has developed into the comprehensive child welfare organisation that it is today.

During the 18th century, there was a small but steady flow of Jewish immigrants from Europe. England was an attractive destination for many reasons: cheap travel from the Continent, an unusual degree of religious tolerance and considerable trade opportunities. Consequently, the Jewish population grew from an estimated 7,000 in 1750 to nearly 25,000 by the end of the century.

Most Jewish immigrants settled in London, a thriving commercial centre with extensive movement of goods, services and people. However, many arrived penniless and unskilled. Unable to afford either education or apprenticeships, they turned to the traditional activities of peddling, hawking or street trading for their precarious survival. A minority resorted to petty crime.

Old Clothes to Sell, print by A.Courcell, c.1820. Jewish immigrants frequently became street traders.

The Piccadilly Nuisance, print by G.Cruikshank, 1818. Among the crowd are reputed to be a Jewish orange vendor, a Jewish boy pickpocket and a Jewess with a basket of fruit.

The Jewish community in 18th century London encompassed considerable variations in wealth and status. It resembled the wider Georgian society where there was a great deal of poverty, very limited public assistance and a recognised problem of crime. The older Sephardi community had developed a network of charitable services, but there was relatively little organised philanthropy in the much larger Ashkenazi community.

Breaking the cycle of poverty and crime

The established Jewish community was embarrassed by the adverse attention that its poor immigrant population attracted. Jewish leaders hoped to improve the standing of Jewish society and break the cycles of poverty and anti-social behaviour through education, job training and moral discipline. It was hoped that if poor Jewish youths were taught trade skills and English manners, they would become productive and respectable members of society.

NVEI TSEDEK - THE JEWS' HOSPITAL

Abraham Goldsmid (1756-1810), print by Richard Dighton. Tucked under the financier's left arm is a list of his charitable contributions.

Among the most influential figures in Anglo-Jewry at the end of the 18th century was Abraham Goldsmid, whose brother Benjamin had been instrumental in establishing the Royal Naval Asylum. In 1795, Abraham - together with his brother - started campaigning for funds for a major Jewish poor relief scheme. Within two years, they had collected £20,000, including donations from non-Jewish banking friends.

In 1807, the Jews' Hospital - *Nvei Tsedek* ('Abode of Righteousness') - was established at Mile End "to uplift the morals and occupations of the young poor" and to keep them out of conversionist and Christian free schools. At that time, the term "hospital" was used to denote a charitable institution that cared for the sick, old or destitute, or housed and educated the needy young.

A small section of the Jews' Hospital was used as an old-age home. The rest served as a boarding trade school for children of respectable poor families - keeping them from the temptations of London street life while training them to be productive citizens.

The Jews' Hospital, Mile End Road, Whitechapel.

Applicants to the school had to satisfy a variety of requirements. The families of applicants had to have lived in the country for at least ten years - a condition designed to discourage additional immigration to Britain - and the parents had to submit their marriage certificates. Applicants had to provide character references, and illegitimate, deserted or destitute Jews were not accepted. They also had to show evidence of good health and be able to read both English and Hebrew. Boys were admitted between the ages of 10 and 12; girls between the ages of 7 and 10.

When the Jews' Hospital enrolled its first residents, it accepted ten boys, eight girls and ten elderly persons. Over the years, the facilities were extended to accommodate an ever increasing number of children.

A total institution

The school was a total institution, with the "inmates" - as the children were referred to - living there on a permanent basis. Discipline was stern, with a heavy emphasis on improving morals and behaviour to make the children a credit to the Anglo-Jewish community. In 1813, a Lady Visitor commented:

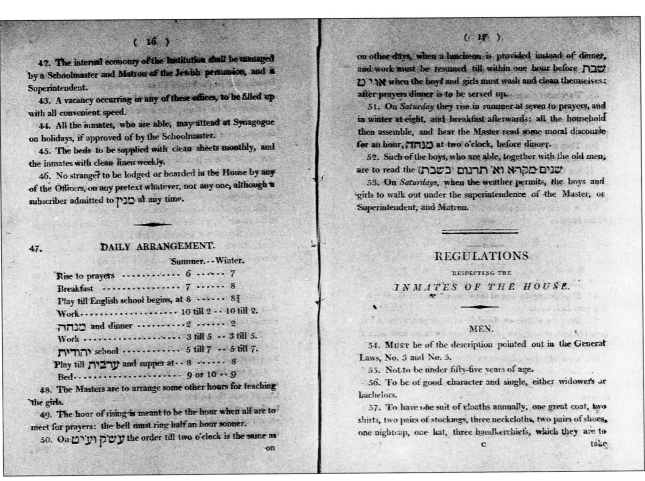

Daily timetable and regulations of the Jews' Hospital, in *Resolutions and Rules*, 1808.

"They have much to unlearn. They, necessarily from their previous situations, bring with them many habits which must be eradicated entirely before they can receive any real education."

At the school, the children's education included practical skills, together with reading, writing and arithmetic. Jewish religious studies comprised a considerable portion of the school day. Morning and afternoon prayers were held daily, and those who failed to attend forfeited their breakfast or evening meal. The children were regularly examined in English and Hebrew.

In the early days, boys were apprenticed to master artisans within the Home to learn shoemaking, chair-making and cabinet-making. Later, they were apprenticed outside the Home and prepared for a wider range of occupations.

"Cabinet Maker" from *The Book of Trades*, published in 1811.

5

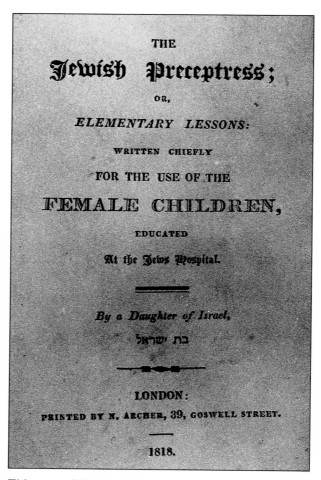

THE

Jewish Preceptress;

OR,

ELEMENTARY LESSONS:

WRITTEN CHIEFLY

FOR THE USE OF THE

FEMALE CHILDREN,

EDUCATED

At the Jews Hospital.

By a Daughter of Israel,

בת ישראל

LONDON:

PRINTED BY N. ARCHER, 39, GOSWELL STREET.

1818.

Title page of *The Jewish Preceptress*, a strict moral guide detailing the duties of girls at the Jews' Hospital, 1818.

Girls were trained in domestic skills, and at 15 they were usually placed in domestic service. In *The Jewish Preceptress*, a book published in 1818 for "female children educated at the Jews' Hospital", girls were reminded of their duties, which included religious observance, gratitude, humility, honesty and industry.

"As most of you, my dear girls! will be servants in respectable families, remember it is the indispensable duty of a servant to be industrious, economical, careful, and attentive. If a servant is lazy and wasteful; if she is impertinent, a liar, or a gossip; she is, in a moral point of view, equally as dishonest as if she had actually committed theft."

REPUTATION AND STRUCTURE

From the beginning, there were great hopes for the Jews' Hospital. After a number of initial problems, it would seem that the institution gradually became well established and well regarded. A popular periodical of 1832, *Guide to Knowledge*, commented:

> "Go to the Jews' Hospital at Mile End and say that in point of regularity, industry and usefulness, has it a superior among the countless institutions of the metropolis."

In the struggle for Jewish emancipation, the Jews' Hospital was cited by David Salomons (later Lord Mayor of London) as "one of their most useful Establishments for the instruction of Jewish Youth in handicraft trades". It was an example of the way the Jews had "anxiously endeavoured to diffuse Education (and instruction in various Mechanical Arts) among their poorer classes". *(A Short Statement on Behalf of his Majesty's subjects Professing the Jewish Religion*, 1835.)

By 1860, the school had acquired the status of an ordinary boarding school, as one Old Boy of the period recalled:

> "I experienced the usual conditions of a big public school... There was popularly no charity taint attached to scholarships at the Jews' Hospital and, in addition to this, there were children there related to some of the best Jewish families in London... I was now what was then known in metropolitan and provincial Jewry as a *Niveh Tzadek* boy, the equivalent of the Blue Coat schoolboy in the Christian community. We had a distinctive uniform, one for weekdays and the other for *Shabbos*, the latter being quite decent and not suggestive of a charity garb."

7

Considerable emphasis was placed on both secular and religious education. In 1861, the Chairman of the Jews' Hospital reported that the school was "the first Jewish Establishment in England which supplied ministers of Religion... and they continue to train youth for the ministry of Religion".

Patronage and leadership

Typical of British charities of the day, the Jews' Hospital drew its leaders from the social elite, including royalty. From 1815, after the death of the Goldsmid brothers, the Duke of Sussex (Queen Victoria's uncle) became the Hospital's Patron. His brother, the Duke of Cambridge, succeeded him in 1843. Royal patronage has continued since that time, and Her Majesty the Queen is the present Patron.

The Duke of Sussex.   Sir Anthony de Rothschild.

In the 19th century, most, if not all, prominent Anglo-Jewish families were associated with the Jews' Hospital. The following report in *The Jewish Chronicle*, describing the 1845 Anniversary Dinner, was typical:

> "HRH the Duke of Cambridge, Patron of the Charity, presided, supported on his right by Baron Anthony de Rothschild and on his left by Sir Moses Montefiore."

Throughout the history of the charity, successive generations of a number of families have continued their association.

An important source of funds for the charity was the Annual Dinner. A major social event for men, it took place at a London tavern. The Patron presided, and the evening

ODE

SPOKEN BY ONE OF THE GIRLS,

AT THE

Anniversary Dinner,

OF THE

JEWS' HOSPITAL,

ON

WEDNESDAY, 10th APRIL, 1867.

CHILDREN of woe, by want and suffering torn,
   Exposed to evil, by our hapless state;
Deserted—friendless—fatherless—forlorn,
   Left to the worst extremities of fate;—

Such were we once; but Oh! how changed our doom;
   To useful arts, to moral habits train'd,
Now in our cheeks do healthful roses bloom—
   Now are our hearts by sorrow unprofaned.

Many perchance, who, left unchecked to sin,
   Had closed their days in some unhallowed strife,
Shall now survive, an honoured name to win,
   And ornament the humble walks of life.

While thus you teach the friendless young to live,
   And with paternal zeal their wants supply,
Others there are, whose aged hands receive
   From you the boon that cheers them as they die.

Oh, may such bounty unremitted flow!
   Speed your own works of charity and love!
And every blessing thus dispensed below,
   Shall gain a tenfold recompense above.

Ode recited by a girl pupil at the Jews' Hospital, praising the institution
at its anniversary fund-raising dinner, 1867.

was replete with toasts. Prodigious quantities of food and drink were consumed.
Beneficiaries of the charity paraded around the room, often accompanied by a banner,
and older children carried samples of shoes and other items that they had made. A
young girl would recite an ode in recognition of the good work of the benefactors, and
entertainments were provided.

THE MOVE TO NORWOOD

The Jews' Hospital at its new site, Lower Norwood, 1863.

By 1860, there were 100 boys and 40 girls enrolled at the Jews' Hospital. Most came from London, with a few from the provinces. Competition for admission was keen, and the buildings had become overcrowded and dilapidated. The choice was either to rebuild or to move.

A new home in the countryside

Barnett and Isabella Meyers presented the Jews' Hospital with eight acres of land in West Norwood, and in 1861, the President of the Orphanage, Sir Anthony de Rothschild, laid the foundation stone. By 1866, the large purpose-built Victorian building was ready.

The new premises could accommodate 220 children. Since elderly residents found the distance from town too great, they were boarded out and received financial support in lieu of accommodation.

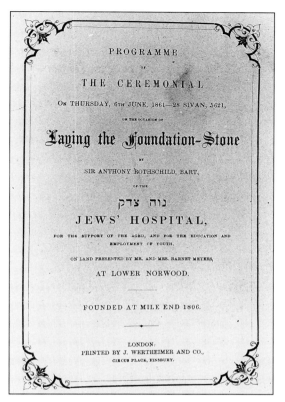

Programme for the laying of the foundation stone
of the Jews' Hospital at Norwood, 6 June 1861.

Poor Street of London, print by Doré, 1872.

There was a trend in the wider community to remove similar institutions from town to country, and the move from the insalubrious metropolis suited the children. A boy arriving at Norwood in the 1870s wrote:

> "Having been born and raised in London, the rosy cheeks of the Norwood boys seemed uncommmon to me and the children themselves looked so healthy."

Improved facilities

The children soon settled into the new building and were quick to appreciate the improvement in their living conditions:

> "What a change from the drab dinginess of Mile End. I remember the big hospitable gates, the broad pathway up to the handsome big building... We had a magnificent lawn big enough for football and its own grounds surrounded by fields."

Facilities at West Norwood included a very large outdoor playground, an underground playground, a dining-hall to accommodate 200 children, school rooms with individual desks - one for the 150 boys and another smaller one for the girls, a library, a large plunging bath, large dormitories, and a synagogue.

> "The synagogue at Norwood was a glory. We had been initiated into everything that smacked of synagogue at Mile End but here was the real thing on a fine scale... A real *shul*, and we loved it!"

The synagogue at the Jewish Orphanage, West Norwood, c. 1930, showing original seating of the 1860s and ark curtains made by Lady Gertrude Spielman in 1912.

Daily life

Each pupil at the Jews' Hospital was assigned an identification number for their possessions. In the early years, teachers addressed the pupils by number, too.

One Old Boy recorded the daily routine at Norwood:

> "We rise at half past six, attend synagogue, breakfast at seven, which consists of bread and butter and milk, and then we prepare ourselves for school from nine to twelve. We have dinner at half past twelve... meat and potatoes... and begin school again at half past two until five. We have our supper at six, which is the same as breakfast. Then we have synagogue again."

A senior girl's daily timetable was very different:

> "In the morning we were in class, and in the afternoons we spent a month in turn either in housework, cooking, sewing, scrubbing, darning, and the whole round of domestic duties."

In the days before modern drugs and hygiene, there was particular concern about the spread of disease. A scholar of the 1860s wrote:

> "Cleanliness was a first law at the institution. Between the physician, nurse and general management we were scrupulously clean. Rules of simple hygiene were pasted on the walls of the school room and in the matter of health we were very carefully supervised."

Discipline was strict. Room 42 was set aside for chronic cases of insubordination but rarely used. In general, the threat of caning or shaming in front of classmates proved a sufficient deterrent.

> "The headmaster inspired fear... He was a terror with the cane, and wielded it with fine facility; with the alternative, his slipper, he was no less similarly perfect in action."

Leisure-time activities were "many, but simple".

> "We enjoyed swings, skipping-ropes, hoops, walks to the Crystal Palace, rambles among the lovely hills, dales and woods of Norwood, Dulwich and Sydenham."

Streatham Common, c.1890. Situated near Norwood, the children regularly went to the Common for their walks.

All the children had regular walks on Streatham Common, and sometimes they went to the Dulwich Picture Gallery. On Saturday afternoons, boys who had sisters in the school were allowed to see them for one hour.

A variety of social backgrounds

Among the great events in the children's lives was the monthly visiting day, when parents and friends visited the Home. For some children, this could be a painful occasion, highlighting variations in their social and economic backgrounds.

> "Sometimes the scenes were pathetic in the extreme. The social conditions of the boys were not equal. Some were the children of the comparatively well-off, others the poorest of the poor. The differences were apparent in many ways - the 'goodies' brought, the pocket-money left, the dress and get-up of the mothers."

> "My father had been a prosperous merchant and we kept five servants. A great commercial failure involved him in ruin and we were in abject want. I well remember my dear mother pawning even the locket with my father's enamelled likeness in order to buy us bread. There were several girls in the school whose parents had been in a similar position, and still more boys."

The backgrounds of the applicants were described in the assessments of the institution's investigators:

> "A splendid case. Parents English. Mother making a splendid fight, but weighed down by the number of children - six. Strongly recommended."

> "Father is a poor hawker... a man of unsteady and thriftless habits... For the sake of the boy it would be desirable to admit."

THE JEWS' ORPHAN ASYLUM

The Jews' Orphan Asylum - the other charitable institution from which Norwood developed - has vague origins, reputedly connected to the 1830 cholera epidemic that killed 5,000 people in London alone and left many children orphaned. One colourful story relates how a poor cucumber seller, Abraham Green, took pity on three children left destitute after their parents died. Carrying two of the children in his arms and leading the third by the hand, he went round the Jewish quarter appealing for money until he had collected a small maintenance fund - source of the Jews' Orphan Asylum.

The Jews' Orphan Asylum was established in Leman Street, London, in 1831. Its purpose was "the maintaining, clothing, educating and apprenticing of Jewish children born in lawful wedlock, deprived of both parents, and for a limited number deprived of one parent only". The Orphan Asylum provided the children with an education, taught them a trade and arranged their apprenticeships.

Vegetable seller, published by S. Marks, c.1830. A street vendor such as this one reputedly raised funds for children orphaned in the 1830 cholera epidemic.

15

Applicants for Admission to a Casual Ward, print by Samuel Fildes, 1874. London's homeless and destitute were not admitted to The Jews' Orphan Asylum until the 1860s and looked elsewhere for support.

Initially, seven children were housed at the Asylum. By 1841, the number had increased to 28. In 1846, thanks to funds donated by Abraham Lyons Moses in memory of his late wife Abigail, new premises were built at Tenter Ground, Goodman's Fields. These housed 40 children admitted between the ages of two and eleven.

Chief Rabbi Nathan Adler.

At the stone-laying for the new building in 1846, Chief Rabbi Nathan Adler said:

> "This charity owes its origin to a few poor and humble men who, at a time of great and desolating calamity, nobly stepped forward and, after the toils of the day were over, gave their time and their mites towards the succour of helpless orphans who, but for their philanthropy, would have been compelled to wander in the streets, destitute of food or home."

The Great Synagogue, London, where a special pew was reserved for the boys of the Jews' Orphan Asylum.

In 1850, the Jews' Orphan Asylum amalgamated with two smaller organisations - the Infant Orphan Charity and the Charity for the Support and Education of Fatherless Children - with the condition that double orphans took precedence over single orphans when vacancies occurred. By 1870, the building at Tenter Ground had been enlarged to accommodate about sixty orphans.

Despite its humble origins, the Orphan Asylum soon involved leading members of the community and received royal patronage that included the Queen Dowager, the Duke of Cambridge and the Duchess of Kent. It also maintained a close relationship with the Great Synagogue, where a special pew was reserved for the boys.

THE JEWS' HOSPITAL AND ORPHAN ASYLUM

Main buildings of the Jews' Hospital and Orphan Asylum, West Norwood, c.1910.

During the early 19th century, Jewish charities proliferated in a haphazard way, much like their English counterparts. There were various attempts to rationalise communal philanthropy.

In 1856, the amalgamation of the Jews' Orphan Asylum and the Jews' Hospital was suggested. However, the two residential homes had very different histories and aims. The Jews' Hospital had been set up by leading members of the Jewish community to provide education for the children of the struggling poor, with an emphasis on producing adults who would be worthy representatives of the Jewish community. By contrast, the Jews' Orphan Asylum started as a grassroots organisation concerned simply with caring for orphans who had no home.

The entrance of the Jews' Hospital and Orphan Asylum, West Norwood, c.1910.
Postcard with Jewish New Year greetings inscribed below in Hebrew.

Eventually, financial problems and inadequate accommodation forced the issue. In 1876, the Jews' Orphan Asylum merged with the Jews' Hospital, becoming the Jews' Hospital and Orphan Asylum. The children from the Jews' Orphan Asylum moved to Norwood, which was half empty at the time because it lacked the funds to accept more children.

Once the amalgamation was completed, the concern of the Jewish community to place children in need of care could be directed exclusively towards this single establishment.

In the following years, the combined institution continued to develop. A workshop was donated and built in the grounds to help the boys gain technical skills and increase their employment opportunities, and a 'modern' laundry was installed to help defray costs and teach girls additional skills.

GROWTH AND ENLARGEMENT

The East End of London was home for many poor immigrant Jews in the late 19th and early 20th centuries.

Pressure for admission intensified toward the end of the 19th century. With large-scale immigration from Eastern Europe, more than twenty per cent of England's Jews was classified as poor and there were ever more families in need. The Home at Norwood expanded rapidly, increasing its intake from 159 Jewish children in 1877 to nearly 260 by 1888. A great many children had to be turned away, and by 1894 plans were under way to extend the premises to accommodate even more children.

Children in the Centenary Hall dining room, Norwood, c.1895.

In 1897, the Home was much enlarged with the opening of the Centenary Hall and new wings, at a cost of £20,000 raised largely by President Sir George Faudel-Phillips, Lord Mayor of London. A final addition in 1911 was the Arnold and Jane Gabriel Home, a pleasant new building in the grounds, specially designed for 50 children aged 5 to 8 years old. Thereafter, the Jews' Hospital and Orphan Asylum at Norwood was able to care for at least 400 children.

Infants at the Gabriel Home, Norwood, c.1911.

There was some debate about the advisability of continually enlarging the institution. As far back as 1869, Sir George Jessel warned the Jews' Orphan Asylum against uncurbed expansion and advocated personal, homely attention for each child. One alternative suggested was 'boarding out', but most Jewish working-class families at the time were large, overcrowded and impoverished, and it was felt that Norwood would give needy children a better start in life.

SELECTING THE CHILDREN

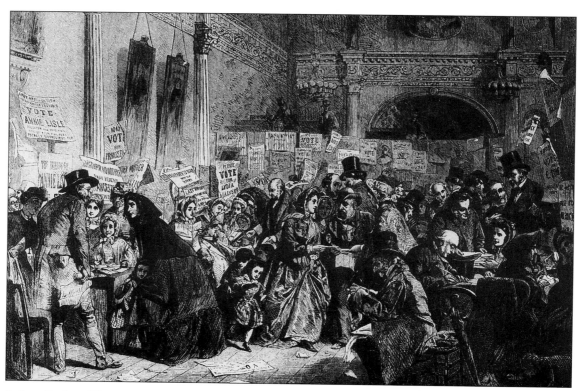

Infant Orphan Election at the London Tavern - Polling, print by G.E.Hicks, 1865.

Following the common pattern of English charities of the time, the Jews' Hospital (and later the Orphan Asylum) was formed as a Voting Charity. Its income depended on voluntary subscriptions, and control was vested in the hands of the subscribers, who voted both in the election of Honorary Officers and in the selection of beneficiaries. The size of a donor's annual subscription determined the number of votes allocated - the larger the subscription, the greater the number of votes and the greater the donor's participation, patronage and power.

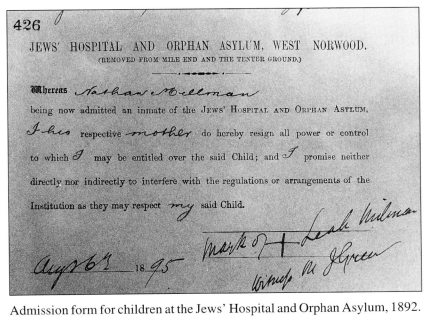

Admission form for children at the Jews' Hospital and Orphan Asylum, 1892.

When vacancies occurred, applicants were first vetted by the Committee. Applicants had to pass educational tests and provide a certificate of their own good conduct and their parents' marriage certificate. Those deemed suitable were submitted for election, which took place twice yearly. Since the applicants' success often depended on knowing people with influence to recommend them, candidates without such influence were often overlooked in favour of less-deserving applicants. However, although the system was clearly unfair, it was retained until 1924 because the Committee feared that changing it could lead to a loss of subscribers.

The Committee was reluctant to accept illegitimate, abandoned or destitute children, since they feared that this would encourage desertion and vice, as well as lowering the tone of the institution. These children were cared for by the Parish Unions. In 1868, under pressure from the Jewish Board of Guardians, the Jews' Hospital changed its admissions policy and started to accept some children from Parish workhouses. Only after the Second World War did it become a working principle that any Jewish child taken into care would be admitted to Norwood.

> נוה צדק
>
> **JEWS' HOSPITAL AND ORPHAN ASYLUM,**
> LOWER NORWOOD.
>
> ---
>
> **JANUARY ELECTION.**
>
> ---
>
> To the GOVERNORS and SUBSCRIBERS
>
> THE favour of your VOTES and interest is respectfully solicited on behalf of SARAH HYMAN, whose mother is dead. If not successful this time, she will be incapacitated for future election, owing to age.
>
> The case is recommended by Lady Rothschild, Rev. M. Keizer, Sydney M. Samuel, Esq., Samuel Montagu, Esq., Dr. A. Asher.
>
> Proxies will be thankfully received by Rev. M. Keizer, 8, Bury-street, Bevis Marks, E.C.; Mr. J. M. Myers, 13, Duke street, Aldgate; and Mr. Asher I. Myers, 43, Finsbury-square.

Notice of the forthcoming election of a child to the Jews' Hospital and Orphan Asylum, *The Jewish Chronicle*, 10 January 1879.

DEVOTED SUPPORTERS

Many men and women have contributed greatly to the development of Norwood. The following individuals are just three outstanding examples of the numerous Committee members who have given their time, energy and funds to serve the organisation.

Dr Henry Behrend.

Dr Henry Behrend (1828-1893)

Dr Henry Behrend became Chairman of the General Committee of the Jews' Hospital in 1868 when it was heavily in debt. Under his careful administration, expenses were brought into realistic alignment with income. Subsequently, as President of the institution, he continued to devote himself to its cause and played a leading part in its progress after amalgamation. The 1894 Annual Report emphasises his contribution:

> "For nearly a quarter of a century, Dr Behrend presided over the Jews' Hospital and (after its amalgamation with the Orphan Asylum) over the present institution. The remarkable progress of the charity is largely due to the great skill and judgement with which he carried on the noble work."

A fine reference library was presented to Norwood in Dr Behrend's memory.

Daniel Marks (1849-1904)

Daniel Marks entered the Jews' Hospital as a child. Subsequently, he secured a commanding position on the Stock Exchange, joined the Jews' Hospital Committee, and became its Treasurer for 22 years. He was devoted to the institution, donating and raising a great deal of money for it. In 1880, he donated a complete gymnasium and games equipment. He contributed to the happiness of the children in innumerable ways, for example providing a yearly Purim feast. Later scholars enjoyed a magnificent iced cake - large enough to serve all the children - given annually in his memory.

Daniel Marks.

Lady Gertrude Spielman.

Lady Gertrude Spielman (1864-1914)

From its earliest days, women played key roles at the Jews' Hospital. The Lady Visitors' Book indicates the active involvement of lady philanthropists from the beginning of the 19th century. In 1854, the institution appointed a Ladies' Committee to help "in the training of the girls and in the domestic arrangements of the Establishment" and many of its members made regular visits to the Home.

In supervising and reforming the day-to-day affairs of Norwood in the late 19th and early 20th century, the name of Gertrude Spielman stands out. She was closely associated with Norwood for half a century, joining the Ladies' Committee in the 1880s and subsequently becoming its Chair.

Mrs. Gabriel's 91st Birthday Party

Mrs Arnold Gabriel, who endowed the Gabriel Home at Norwood, celebrates her 91st birthday with the children of the Home, 1930. With her are Lady Gertrude Spielman and Mr and Mrs Kaye, Headmaster and Matron of the Home.

While the contributions of Gertrude Spielman and other women were appreciated by Norwood - especially in fund-raising activities - it was not until 1901 that women were permitted to join the General Committee. Lady Spielman was in the forefront of the campaign to gain admission for women to that committee, on which she later served. Over the years, she served on many other committees, was a school manager and became a Vice-President of Norwood.

LIFE AT NORWOOD

Norwood's imposing entrance hall with its white marble staircase, c.1895.

The Jews' Hospital and Orphan Asylum, or Norwood as it was commonly known, was warmly regarded within the Jewish community and had a high reputation in the wider community. On 16 April 1897, *The Jewish Chronicle* reported that Norwood aimed to "turn out children with the same education, the same habits, and the same chances in life as any other well-cared for, well-taught, English boys and girls".

A great step forward was taken in 1900 when the school came under the Education Department, leading to improved standards of teaching and added status for the teachers.

In 1928, the institution changed its name to The Jewish Orphanage. At the time, the term "orphan" was used in child care not only to describe a child with no parents but, in the broader sense used by Dr Barnardo, to encompass children with both parents dead, one parent dead or both parents unsuitable or unable to care for the child. In fact, in 1928, only 55 of the children were orphans in the full sense, while 198 were fatherless, 115 motherless and 16 had both parents living. In many cases, a parent had been widowed and did not have sufficient resources to keep all their offspring at home.

Outdoor infants' class, Norwood, c.1912.

"I was ten years old when my grandfather took me from the East End... My brother was already there. I had four sisters. My mother had died and my father was a presser. He couldn't keep the children... There was no help from the State, no Social Services."

"My mother died when I was seven months old. My father remarried in 1927, when I was three or four, and my stepmother had 11 children. It must have been very difficult for my father to have managed 17 children, so I was put into care."

Counteracting institutionalisation

As concepts of child care changed, and as the institution became ever larger, there was growing concern about the adverse effects of institutionalisation, and great efforts were made to counteract monotony and to make life more pleasant. An important influence in this direction was Meyer Kaye, Headmaster of Norwood from 1910 to 1936. He was a man of many talents and great organisational ability who played a vital role in the development of the Orphanage. His wife, Esther, acted as matron.

A report of a member of the Children's Branch of the Home Office, included in Norwood's 1931 Annual Report, commented on the Home's informal atmosphere.

> "We were struck by the absence of red tape, the complete lack of any sign of repression and the absolute naturalness of the children - 350 children dined in one Hall at tables holding 20 each - there was none of the lining up and marching into place which one usually finds in large institutions of this kind. Innumerable societies exist for the boys and girls, managed almost entirely by themselves - choral, literary, dramatic, boxing, debating and musical societies".

Arrival at Norwood

In her autobiography, Sheila Graham recalls her first day at Norwood, circa 1910:

> "Newcomers - boys and girls - were herded into a bathroom with steaming water in three big tubs. They were told to remove their clothes, which were then handled gingerly and put in three small piles... The boys were staring at the girls and whispering and giggling. Before the bath, three to a tub, the girls as well as the boys were sheared to the scalp by a woman with strong clippers. Some of the girls cried... After the bath, they were all dressed alike, in washed-out blue rompers with small knickers attached. And now you could not distinguish boy from girl."

Some children found it difficult to adjust to institutional life, but others were excited at the prospect.

> "It seemed a complete new environment with opportunities. The fact that my older brother was there gave me the opportunity of being with him and a new start."

Daily life

In the 1924 issue of the Old Girls' Guild Magazine, Gertrude Spielman recalled Norwood as she first knew it 40 years earlier:

> "When I cast my thoughts back to Norwood as I first knew it, it was smaller in size, more conventional in character and the girls were only taught school subjects and rarely went beyond the school gates except to walk two-and-two in serpent fashion. That was the rule of all schools ... Hockey, cricket and all organised outdoor games for girls were unknown in those days - they would have been considered too rough, unmannerly, nay dangerous. The small girls depended upon skipping ropes and rubber balls,

Girls' hockey team, Norwood, c.1911.

and the elder girls found joy in endless crochet work... In fact, both children and staff were dependent one upon the other for devising amusements, and were thus drawn together in more intimate fashion than obtains under modern conditions."

Children at the Orphanage found their days ordered into a tight schedule, punctuated by the ringing of the school bell, which created order and ritual.

Boys' class, Norwood, c.1912.

"Four hundred and fifty children would rise at 6.30... rush down to breakfast, inspection and roll-call, daily lessons, daily leisure time."

Morning assemblies were another feature of daily life at Norwood:

"When you went to assemblies, you had to stand according to your numbers, starting from number one. I was number 36, in the third or fourth row. The teacher used to call out your number and you had to answer to see if you were there. If you had a query, you had to tell the teacher. If your boots were too tight, they gave you a bigger size... We also had to recite the *Shema*."

Leisure activities

A wide range of leisure activities was encouraged. To quote Gertrude Spielman, writing in 1924:

Norwood boys' club, 1920s.

"Bit by bit changes have crept in, and in their train what a vista of improvements and increasing opportunities! School clubs, hobby evenings, organised games, debates, gramophone concerts, with vision of wireless and cinema installations looming large, provide such a choice as fell to the lot of no child in former days."

A former pupil recollects:

"The older girls were appointed 'guardians' to the younger ones and were responsible not only for darning their own black woollen stockings but also those of their 'slutty charges' - as we called them! We also had letter-writing evenings to write home and hobby evenings with leather-work

31

Norwood girls at play, c.1910.

classes, indoor games and the very popular 'operetta' classes which I am sure encouraged many of us to develop a love of music."

Mr Kaye encouraged the children to leave the Orphanage for outings to local parks and places of interest such as the Dulwich Art Gallery and Crystal Palace. He reminded all the boys and girls that their outings were an honour and a responsibility, and concluded a long list of written advice on safety and courtesy with the following:

"Remember that you will be exposed to temptation when you pass or enter shops where small articles such as fruit, toys, etc. are displayed. You must learn to resist such temptations if you wish to grow up into an honest boy or girl. Any departure from the strict code of honesty will bring disgrace not only to yourself, but also on your family, your school and on the Jewish name."

Growing up at Norwood

The youngest children at Norwood - aged from five to eight years old - were cared for in Gabriel Home.

"I went to Norwood when I was seven years old in 1920. I was in the Gabriel Home. I used to wet my bed so Nurse Jessie took me to the loo every night. One Thursday night on the way back to bed, she said to me, 'Would you like to see the fireworks on display at Crystal Palace?' She stood me on the window sill in my nightie. I have never forgotten those fireworks and I never needed to be taken to the loo again."

The Gabriel Home, built in 1911 for the youngest children at Norwood.

When the children left Gabriel Home, they moved into dormitories in the main house. The largest dormitory was vast, with 78 beds in three rows.

"It was like a great, big hospital."

There was a separate dormitory for children who wet their beds and a third dormitory in the girls' section for girls who had begun to menstruate.

"Once it happened to me, I told the headmistress. They put your name down and you went to a different dormitory because they liked us all to be together and they called us 'big girls'."

Norwood staff, c.1930.

When the children moved into the main house and started school, they had to take on more responsibility and do jobs in the Home.

> "Everyone had a little job to do before school. You might be sweeping part of the top playground, cleaning brass, tidying the synagogue."

High days and holidays

From the time of the Jews' Hospital, the Jewish festivals had always been highlights of the school year - in particular Passover and *Succoth*. *Barmitzvahs* were also very special occasions.

Norwood boys on an outing to Margate, c.1911.

Sports day and prize day were other annual highlights and, from the early days in the East End, benefactors had made it possible for the children to go on a variety of outings. Some of these - such as the zoo and the pantomime - became regular and eagerly anticipated yearly treats, and in later years, a special train was laid on for the 20-minute journey to the theatre. An outing to Olympia was followed by a slap-up high tea with fish and chips and ice cream.

When in 1900 Norwood came under the Education Department, the school closed for three weeks every summer. Soon after, a holiday home at Margate was presented by Isaac Davis, and from 1904 onwards the children were able to enjoy a holiday there. This was just the start of a variety of breaks provided for those children who remained in residence over the holidays.

> "Holidays were a great time for those of us who 'stayed behind'. There was the JFS hut at Seaforth and the Girl Guide camps for girls and the JLB

Girls leaving Norwood for their annual outing to Margate, c.1911.

camps for the boys. Pictures twice a week at the old Norwood Palace, and later at the Regal. I remember when it opened and we saw our first 'talkies'. Then there were the concerts at Brockwell Park, and the mad scramble back afterwards - to be rewarded with sweets when we arrived."

Family contacts

At first, no more than two members of a single family were accepted into Norwood. Later on, the number was increased to three. Brothers and sisters could only meet on one afternoon a week.

Brothers and sisters meet at Norwood, 1910.

"Every Saturday afternoon, boys who had sisters could come over for an hour to visit them, but if I must tell the truth, after greeting their sisters with a preliminary kiss, they seemed to be engrossed in conversation with the other boys' sisters and quite forgot their own."

Relatives waiting to be admitted to Norwood on visiting day, 1910.

There had always been a degree of home visiting, but in 1922 regular home visits were instituted whereby children would go home for a period of a month, if the homes were considered suitable.

Parents and relatives could visit the children for two hours one Sunday afternoon a month. For children without families, visiting day was dreaded.

A child hugs her visiting grandmother, Norwood, 1910.

"To us, it was the worst day of the month and we used to go and hide ourselves. We just felt so out of place. There were some kind people, though, who used to ask to see all the children who had no one to visit them... I was ashamed to go over. My sister and I decided we didn't want charity."

Looking Back

For some children, the orphanage at Norwood represented security and companionship, while others have recollections of unhappiness and repression.

"At Norwood, I had everything given to me. I was lying on clean sheets. I was being fed... It was better than living at home because I was being looked after and my mother had no worry over me."

"Only years later I realised that I had never been cuddled... The authorities were too involved in looking after us to give us the individual love and attention an orphan craves."

"You just had to learn to control your emotions and not to be a cry-baby."

"Of course, not all my memories of Norwood were happy ones, but I prefer to only think of the pleasant ones!"

One child wrote following her return from Norwood to live at home:

"You cannot realise how much I miss you all. After being at Norwood for so long a period, it is very hard to get into the ways of home life - noisy, but nothing like the merry noise and din at Norwood."

Norwood children on a summer holiday party to Essex, 1932.

Many lifelong friendships were established at Norwood, and girls often met for holiday reunions - such as here in Broadstairs, c.1936.

Looking back, a former pupil wrote:

"Like all childhoods, my sojourn (at Norwood) entailed many happy times, as well as fewer, not quite so happy. All in all, I can truthfully say I am proud to have been a 'Norwood boy' - the standard of education bestowed on us has served me in very good stead throughout my life."

EMPLOYMENT AND AFTERCARE

From its inception, the primary objective of the Jews' Hospital was to prepare the children to become respectable and useful citizens.

Boys

In 1883, an Aftercare Committee was established, with each member acting as 'guardian' to supervise the welfare of a few school-leavers. The conviction that the success of the Orphanage was reflected in the achievements of the children after they left Norwood led to the growth in importance of the Committee's work.

For many years, the Aftercare Committee was chaired and led by Sir Basil Henriques, a prominent social worker and magistrate known especially for his work with boys' clubs and juvenile delinquents. Connected to Norwood for over forty years, he outlined the duties of the Committee in a 1928 report:

1. To place the boys in suitable homes.
2. To find work that fits the boys and not the boy that fits the work, which is the great temptation in these times of unemployment.
3. To watch and educate his character.

In the early days, all the boys were apprenticed. As production processes changed, there were fewer industrial apprenticeships and not all boys were suited to such pursuits. Instead, the children entered a greater variety of occupations. Engineering, dental mechanics, fancy leather goods making, furniture making, hairdressing, office and warehouse work and jobs in the clothing trades were among those mentioned in the Annual Reports of the late 1920s.

Carpentry workshop at The Jewish Orphanage, 1930s.

In an attempt to encourage boys to leave the East End and move into areas with greater employment opportunities, three hostels for apprentices were established outside London in the late 19th century. However, by 1911, the hostels were closed through lack of use. They were seen as a continuation of institutional life. Instead, efforts were made to board boys out in suitable homes.

Apprentices' hostel in Stoke-on-Trent, opened in 1896.

For boys who spent so much of their childhood together at Norwood, the bonds of friendship were strong and enduring.

> "We were bonded together. We were forced to live together for so many years. Consequently, I have many friends who are old Norwood scholars... The ones of my period are closer than after the war."

Girls

The aims of the aftercare service for girls were basically the same as for boys. From the early days of the Jews' Hospital, a few girls were apprenticed to tradesmen such as furriers and bead-workers. Some "suitable girls with talent" were trained as nursery governesses, but choices were very limited and the majority went into domestic work.

By the end of the 19th century, there was a trend away from domestic service. The girls preferred the independence of trades such as cap-making, cigar-making and tailoring, despite their low pay.

The Ladies' Committee - later to become the Aftercare Committee (Girls) - acted as guardians, supervising all aspects of the girls' welfare for the first few years after they left the institution.

> "When we left, every child was given a *Singer's Prayer Book* as well as a big tin trunk and a new outfit of clothes."

A cookery class in the kitchen at Norwood, c.1896.

The Aftercare Committees supervised the welfare of children - both boys and girls - who won scholarships to other schools and either returned to their homes or boarded with families nearby.

Members of the Aftercare Committee also arranged for the girls to have medical treatment and holidays, as well as encouraging them to join Girls' Clubs, evening classes and the Old Girls' Guild.

In addition, from 1901, a Visitor was employed to help the girls find jobs - and accommodation if they did not return to their family homes or go into service - when they left Norwood.

The Committee members encouraged the girls to enter domestic service, fearing that with increased freedom the girls "would soon forget the careful training which they received at Norwood". Despite their efforts, by the late 1920s, the girls had all turned to occupations such as dress-making, hairdressing, office and shop work.

The experience of growing up at the Orphanage had a deep impact on some of the women.

> "I've always had to fight my own battles... I had no 'background'. I went out with plenty of boys but when they found out that I had no background they don't actually say but you know in your heart that is why they don't want to be serious with you."

THE ORPHAN AID SOCIETIES

The Jews' Hospital and Orphan Asylum obtained financial support from donations, legacies, fundraising dinners and public appeals. Nevertheless, it remained in deficit. The Orphan Aid Society movement became an additional source of both income and influence.

The Orphan Aid Society movement started with the East London Orphan Aid Society, founded in 1890 to collect funds for the Jews' Hospital and Orphan Asylum. A society with similar aims had been established in Birmingham two years earlier, and soon there were a number of other societies throughout the country.

By 1926, the Orphan Aid Societies provided one third of Norwood's ordinary expenditure. They grew in strength, particularly in metropolitan areas, gaining representation on the Committee and playing an important part in the administration of the Orphanage.

Norwood encouraged the support of the societies by inviting their representatives to make annual visits to the Home. Every Sunday during the summer months, a different society visited the Orphanage. The tea party and pastries were a welcome treat for the children.

Lewis Levy, founder of the Orphan Aid Society in 1890. The organisation provided a major source of funding and influence for the Jews' Hospital and Orphan Asylum.

East London Orphan Aid Society.

Founded for the purpose of augmenting the funds of the Jewish Orphanage, West Norwood.

SYNAGOGUE CHAMBERS,
RECTORY SQUARE, STEPNEY GREEN,
LONDON, E. 1.

Dear Sir, or Madam,　　　　　　　　　　　　　*June 12th, 1936.*

I am directed to invite you to attend the ANNUAL MEETING of the Subscribers to this Charity, which will be held at **THE JEWISH ORPHANAGE,** West Norwood, on SUNDAY, JULY 5th.

Adult Members are to assemble at the Institution from 3 to 3.30 p.m.

The General Meeting will be held from 3.30 to 4.30 p.m.

The Institution will be open for Inspection by the Visitors from 5 to 5.30 p.m.

The Chair will be taken by Mr. S. STEPHANY (President). at 3.30 p m.

AGENDA :

To receive Report of the progress of the Society for the past year.

To receive Statement of Income and Expenditure during the past year. (As annexed.)

To elect Hon. Officers and Committee for current year.
Nominations must be sent in writing to the Hon. Secretary seven days previous to the General Meeting.
In the event of a contest, the poll will be open from 3.30 to 4.30 p.m.

To present Certificates of Life Governorships drawn at previous meeting

To ballot for Life Governorships

And for such other business as may occur.

TO FACILITATE ARRANGEMENTS AT THE INSTITUTION IT IS REQUESTED THAT MEMBERS WHO INTEND TO BE PRESENT WILL PLEASE REPLY TO ME AT ONCE.

I am, dear Sir, or Madam,

Yours faithfully,

MYRA L. STEPHANY, Hon. Sec.,
5, Albemarle Mansions, N.W. 3.

New members can participate in the ballot by paying 2/2 (six months' subscription).

COLLECTING BOXES for the East London Orphan Aid Society can be obtained on application to the Hon. Secretary, or the Collector, Mr. S. Hart, 96, Exmouth Street, Stepney, E. I.

A Cricket Match will be played on the Lawn during the Afternoon.

Notice for the Annual Meeting of the East London Orphan Aid Society, 1936.

Another innovative source of support for the Orphanage came from the Children's Orphan Aid Society. Inaugurated at the end of the 19th century by the Chief Rabbi and affiliated to a number of the larger synagogues, the society encouraged children to subscribe a penny a week to the charity as a lesson in civic and religious responsibility.

EVACUATION

For the generation of children who were at Norwood at the outbreak of the Second World War, life underwent a sudden and dramatic change - never to be the same again.

Four Norwood boys and the family with whom they were billeted during the Second World War. Hertford, 1940.

Children from Norwood's Gabriel Home hold gifts from US Army personnel during their evacuation. Hertford, c.1940.

Children who were used to living in an institution - insulated, isolated and knowing little of life in the outside world and religions other than Judaism - suddenly found themselves billeted in private homes in the wider community.

Culture shock

"They taught us a lot about Columbus and the Gold Coast but nothing about other people's religions, and being institutionalised it came as a very harsh cultural shock... I think I realised for the first time that people could eat pork and bacon without dying."

Alone, in twos or in groups, they were billeted first in homes around Worthing and later in Hertford. School premises were taken over and the children came together for Hebrew lessons and school subjects. However, the staff was changing, teachers moving on and younger house masters being called up. Much of the sense of community, family and security that Norwood represented was lost.

The children were billeted in homes that varied greatly in class and culture. They adopted the lifestyle of the families they stayed with - for example, eating rabbit stew and going to church with 'Mom' and 'Pops' - and many former best friends became estranged from one another.

The children from this period have many vivid memories.

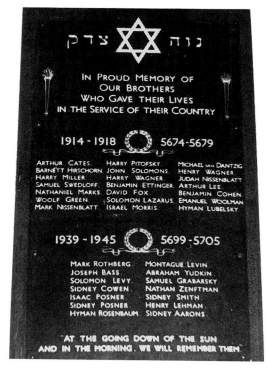

Memorial to those who gave their lives in the service of their country during the First and Second World Wars.

"The American forces came and brought us presents - they brought me the only doll I ever owned."

"War was a blessing - being at Worthing was like a perpetual holiday."

"I was very unhappy at one billet in Hertford. I ran away but my mother brought me back and they found me another. The man of the family taught me all about the countryside. He took me out with him."

AFTER THE WAR

Aerial view of Norwood, c.1951.

The Second World War not only changed the lives of the children who had been at Norwood. It also changed attitudes and ideas about how to care for them when they returned there after war-time evacuation. The Committee was determined to give the children as normal an unbringing as possible.

The most immediate post-war change was to send the children to local schools. Before the war, children had been educated on the Orphanage premises but this policy was not resumed. Contact with the community was further increased by sending the children to local synagogue classes and arranging for them to visit private families.

During the post-war period, many changes were gradually introduced within the Home itself. The children were divided into small, mixed-age, single-sex 'family

Post-war "family tables" in the dining room. Norwood, c.1952.

groups' under the care of a houseparent. Each group of six to eight children was allocated its own table in the dining room and its own 'family room'.

Restrictions on the number of siblings accepted were lifted, and family and friends who had to queue up for their monthly visits in the past were given unrestricted access.

Refurbishing Norwood

The Home needed a complete overhaul, as it had been used for other purposes during the war.

Girls' sitting room at Norwood, 1949.